How to Speak Dog

Dog Training Simplified for Dog Owners

Amy Morford

This book is dedicated to Hannibal, my first German Shepherd and training partner. My knowledge and passion for training dogs would never have developed if it hadn't been for him.

Gone but never forgotten.

Copyright © 2014 by Speedy Publishing LLC

All rights reserved. No part of this publication may be reproduced, distributed or transmitted in any form or by any means, including photocopying, recording, or other electronic or mechanical methods, without the prior written permission of the publisher, except in the case of brief quotations embodied in critical reviews and certain other noncommercial uses permitted by copyright law. For permission requests, write to the publisher, addressed "Attention: Permissions Coordinator," at the address below.

Speedy Publishing LLC (c) 2014
40 E. Main St., #1156
Newark, DE 19711
www.speedypublishing.co

Ordering Information:
Quantity sales; Special discounts are available on quantity purchases by corporations, associations, and others. For details, contact the "Special Sales Department" at the address above.

-- 1st edition

Manufactured in the United States of America

Table of Contents

Publisher's Notes i

Chapter 1: Basic Obedience Training 1

Chapter 2: Understanding Dog Behavior 10

Chapter 2.1: Dog Aggression 11

Chapter 2.2: Separation Anxiety 15

Chapter 2.3: Nuisance Barking 19

Chapter 2.4: Submissive Urination 24

Chapter 2.5: Fear Biting 27

Chapter 2.6: Digging 31

Chapter 3: Clicker Training 34

Chapter 3.1: Tips On How To Use Clicker Training 35

Chapter 4: Get to Crate Training 39

Chapter 5: The Art Of Positive Reinforcement 43

Chapter 6: Best Training Tips by Breed 48

Meet the Author 52

More Books by Amy Morford 53

Publisher's Notes

Disclaimer

This publication is intended to provide helpful and informative material. It is not intended to diagnose, treat, cure, or prevent any health problem or condition, nor is intended to replace the advice of a physician. No action should be taken solely on the contents of this book. Always consult your physician or qualified health-care professional on any matters regarding your health and before adopting any suggestions in this book or drawing inferences from it.

The author and publisher specifically disclaim all responsibility for any liability, loss or risk, personal or otherwise, which is incurred as a consequence, directly or indirectly, from the use or application of any contents of this book.

Any and all product names referenced within this book are the trademarks of their respective owners. None of these owners have sponsored, authorized, endorsed, or approved this book.

Always read all information provided by the manufacturers' product labels before using their products. The author and publisher are not responsible for claims made by manufacturers.

Print Edition 2014

CHAPTER 1: BASIC OBEDIENCE TRAINING

Part of being a responsible dog owner is teaching a pet basic obedience commands. A well-behaved dog makes the difference between a dog owner and a *good* dog owner. Everyone enjoys a well-behaved, well-mannered dog. Teaching your dog basic obedience is a must if you plan to go out in public with your pet. Obedience training will also make visiting your home more enjoyable for friends and family.

It's important that dog owners understand that basic dog obedience training requires a lot of time, repetition and patience. With the right attitude, the training experience will build trust and strengthen the bond between you and your dog.

As an owner it is your responsibility to learn and understand the basic aspects of dog training. This can be accomplished through books, videos, at-home training programs, or structured group or private training classes. Regardless of which learning method is chosen, the owner must implement and follow through with his or her new found knowledge in order for the dog to benefit.

Any dog can successfully learn basic obedience commands. Some dogs and some breeds learn faster than others. Prior to the start of any basic obedience training, the owner should have realistic expectations. No matter how intelligent the dog is, the dog won't learn every command after just a few attempts.

Positive reinforcement is a popular method of training, and it is recommended. Positive reinforcement simply rewards positive and desired behavior through the use of food, toys, verbal praise and affection.

Food is the easiest item to reward your dog with because it can be given in very small amounts and can be carried or concealed in pockets.

Some dogs do not respond well to food. If this is your dog, you need to adjust your training tactics. What makes your dog tick? Is it a particular toy? Find a toy that your dog loves. Put the toy away and bring it out only for training purposes. Implement the toy in your training instead of food.

When setting out for your first training session, it is a good idea to choose a place that doesn't have any distractions (such as other animals or kids). As your dog progresses and regularly responds to commands, it will be important to test your dog by training in places that have distractions.

Remember to keep training sessions short and upbeat. You want your dog to think that training is fun. Always find a way to end the training session with a positive experience for your dog.

Let's start teaching your dog some basic manners. A well-behaved, well-trained dog should respond to some basic commands such as sit, down, heel, stay and come.

Sit

The sit command is one of the most useful and easiest commands you can teach a dog. This is one of the first commands that should be taught. You will need training treats to teach this command.

1. If you have a puppy or a small breed dog, get down to your dog's level by kneeling or sitting. Standing over your dog is a form of dominance and can cause fear or anxiety in some dogs. You want your dog to obey commands because he or she wants to please you, not because the dog is intimidated or fearful.

2. Hold a treat in your hand and let your dog sniff the treat. Do not speak. Slowly move the treat over your dog's head, forcing your dog's head back and its chin up. This will naturally move your dog into the sitting position.

3. As soon as your dog moves into the sitting position, say "sit" and reward your dog with the treat. Continue to calmly praise your dog with "good sit," "good sit." In the beginning stages of training, only use the sit command when your dog is actually sitting.

4. It is important that your dog associates the activity of sitting with the treat, the praise, and with the desired action of sitting. Do not fumble with the treats; the treat needs to happen as your dog is sitting. Work on your timing.

5. Repeat this exercise a few times a day.

6. If your dog is not very food motivated, practice before mealtimes when your dog is hungry.

7. As your dog begins to understand the sit command, gradually decrease the size of the treat. When your dog is sitting consistently, scale back on the treats. Do this by alternating between enthusiastic verbal praise and dishing out treats. Keep your dog guessing.

8. Expose your dog to the "sit" command in different environments and new situations. Practice around people, other dogs, at the park, when the doorbell rings, etc. When practicing in new environments or situations go back to basics and use a lot of treats along with verbal reinforcement. Scale back on the treats as your dog's confidence grows.

Once you have mastered the sit command, you are ready to conquer other basic commands such as down, heel, stay, and come.

Down

The training techniques you learned for the sit command (reward, praise, timing, repetition, and exposure) will be used for every new command you teach your dog. With each new command your confidence and training skills will improve.

Teaching the down command is a natural progression from the sit command.

1. Kneel beside or in front of your dog.

2. Instruct your dog to sit but do not reward your dog.

3. Hold a treat in front of your dog's nose and move it down to the ground in front of your dog.

4. If your dog breaks from the sitting position, start over with the sit command.

5. Repeat this process until your dog goes from the sit position into the down position.

6. Immediately say the command "down" and reward.

7. Follow up with positive verbal reinforcement: "good down."

Dogs generally pick up the down command quickly. Work on this command until your dog can perform it without any assistance or cues from you.

Heel

Teaching a dog to heel will require the use of a corrective collar, a six foot lead and training treats. Hold the lead in your left hand and always have slack in the lead.

1. The correct heeling position for all dogs is to the left of the owner.

2. A dog's shoulder should always remain even with its owner's left leg.

3. If a dog attempts to rush forward or pull ahead this called forging and it is unacceptable.

4. When a dog forges, the owner should get the dog back into place as both continue moving.

5. As soon as your dog moves ahead of you, make an abrupt right hand turn, give a firm correction with the lead and give the command "heel." These three actions need to all occur at the same time.

6. When your dog is back in the proper heeling position give verbal praise: "good heel." Come to a stop and give the sit command at the same time.

7. Immediately reward your dog with a treat and verbal praise.

When your dog forges, you must immediately establish that you control the walk and not your dog. You do this by making sharp right hand turns or reversing directions. Always give a forceful correction and the heel command. This teaches your dog that moving ahead of you is not a rewarding or pleasurable experience.

The first few times you implement a right turn, your dog may stop and pull back away from you. Your dog is expressing that he is unsure what you want from him and going into a flight response. Don't panic and do not give another correction. Pat your leg, call him to you encouragingly and trot or skip a few steps to get him to come forward on his own. Your dog will immediately recover and you should remain low-key and nonchalant over the incident. Your dog will overcome this initial response as he learns the correct behavior and is positively rewarded.

When first starting out, keep the heeling distance from point A to point B short so that rewards are frequent and heeling is a more positive training experience than a negative one. For example: heel for four steps and stop. As you are preparing to stop give the sit command. Reward, praise and do this a few more times. End the session and play. Build off of each session until you have a well-mannered leash partner.

Stay

Teaching your dog to stay is a valuable and useful command. Teaching a hand command along with the verbal command is optional, and is easy to implement in the training process. You will need a training collar, a six-foot lead and training treats.

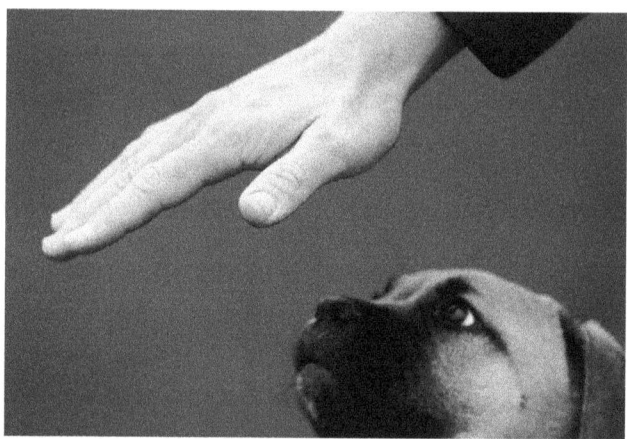

1. Stand next to your dog in the heel position and have your dog sit.

2. Hold the lead in your left hand, and place your right hand in front of your dog's face. Give the command "stay."

3. Step in front of your dog (face your dog) and repeat the command.

4. Reward with a treat and verbal praise: "good stay."

5. Return to the heel position and reward with food and praise.

6. If your dog breaks from the sitting position, start over.

When your dog has mastered this, it is time to increase the difficulty and move to the next step.

7. Follow steps 1–3 and then take two steps back from your dog while holding the lead loosely.

8. Give the command "stay" and hold your right hand out in front of you with your palm facing the dog.

9. Reinforce the behavior with verbal praise: "good stay."

10. Return to your dog and reward with food and praise.

11. If your dog breaks from the sitting position, start over.

This is the basic technique to train your dog to stay. From the sitting and down positions gradually move to the end of the leash. When your dog has accomplished this, put him in a stay and walk back and forth and around him in a large circle. If he turns to keep a visual on you this is okay as long as he stays in place and does not come to you.

To fool-proof your dog's stay, you will need a longer lead and a helper. Attach the lead to the collar and have your helper stand behind your dog while holding the lead but allowing slack. Give your hand signal and stay command and put some distance and distraction into the mix. If your dog breaks from the stay position, your helper will prevent him or her from getting very far. Return to your dog and start the exercise over.

Continue to practice this until you are happy with your dog's stay.

Come

Now that your dog knows how to stay, you can teach him to come to you when called. This command is handy when your dog is outside and you want him inside, or when he has a skunk cornered in your yard and is about to get sprayed á la Pepé le Pew.

You will need a training collar, a six-foot lead and training treats.

1. Put your dog on the lead and put him in a stay position.

2. Face your dog and take two steps backwards away from him.

3. Hold the treat in your hand at waist level.

4. Look your dog in the eyes and give the come command.

5. As you give the command, take one step backwards and use the lead for assistance if needed.

6. (When training this command, I like to make my dog sit after coming, but this step is optional.)

7. Reward your dog with food and praise.

Repeat this process gradually, increasing the distance between you and your dog.

Basic dog obedience training is a learning process for both you and your dog. Always use positive reinforcement and be consistent. Be patient and never express anger towards your dog's reaction to a command. We all learn new things at our own pace.

CHAPTER 2: UNDERSTANDING DOG BEHAVIOR

Your dog's behavior is a direct reflection of you as the pet owner. An untrained dog can become a nuisance to its owner and a danger to others. Unwanted dog behaviors can stem from environmental issues and a lack of training. Dog training is an ongoing process, and behavioral issues need to be addressed as soon as they begin. Let's look into understanding why dogs behave the way they do, the signs, and how to correct the behavior.

CHAPTER 2.1: DOG AGGRESSION

Learn the Signs

One of the worst things a dog owner can face is the fact that their dog has just bitten or attacked someone. Research has shown that one half of the claims made on homeowner's insurance in the last few years were for dog bites. Here are some facts about dog bites:

Approximately 70% of dog bites occur with children and the elderly.

40% of dog bites to children are to the face.

90% of dog bites are to people who know the dogs.

There are two reasons why dogs are aggressive.

1. Poor breeding
2. Not properly socialized

Most people do not want their dogs to be aggressive. There are early warning signs to look for in your dog. Knowing the reason for your dog's aggression is crucial.

There are typically four categories of dog aggression.

Domination

You should be able to detect this pretty quickly. The dominant dog is typically the one that wants to be in control of everything. Many people have the idea that this only manifests in larger breed dogs, but small dogs have this trait as well, and they do bite people. So how do you control this type of aggression?

Rules and structure need to be implemented to prevent dominance from manifesting or reoccurring.

Dogs by nature are pack animals, and a naturally dominate dog will want to lead the pack. You as the owner must assert yourself as the pack leader or the "alpha dog."

The dog has to be taught that you are in charge. The family is the pack, and the dog must learn that his place is simply as a member of that pack. If everyone in the household follows the rules you have set and they do not allow the dog to do things outside of those rules, the dog will quickly understand who is really in charge.

The next thing that you have to do as an owner is to keep the punishments consistent when the dog does something wrong. That being said, rewards also need to be consistent for good behavior. In some instances, professionals may advise to have your dog neutered/spayed to reduce the level of aggression.

Territorial

There are certain breeds of dog that are much more aggressive than others. In many cases people want aggressive dogs to protect their property. The key to this is, training your dog to only be aggressive in the correct circumstances and this requires specialized training. Your dog needs to be aware at all times that you are in charge and that you give the commands. Obedience and protection training is ideal. Your dog needs to learn that when you are away, he is in control. And if an intruder enters the home, that is the time to be aggressive. On the other hand, when you are home, your dog needs to know that you are in charge, and all orders should come from you.

Aggression as a Result of Fear

When a dog is scared, it does what is naturally instinctive - it bites. This can be one of the more difficult aggressive behaviors to curb. It takes a lot of work, but it can be done. The key is to teach the dog not to be fearful. Start by getting a muzzle for the dog. Then start desensitization training. Take the dog on walks where there are many other people and animals until the dog starts to become more social and comfortable in new surroundings.

Bear in mind that the fear the dog is exhibiting could be the result of abuse it may have been subjected to from a previous owner. That is why it is important to find out as much as you can about any dog before you purchase or adopt it. Over time, with the proper training these dogs can overcome fear aggression-but as an owner you should always be cautious and take preventative measures.

Certain breeds are more aggressive in nature and sometimes do not make the best options for pets, especially if children are in the home. Always do your homework and research a breed before bringing home a new pet.

Prey Aggression

Some dogs are born hunters, and this type of dog will use any opportunity to chase down prey. Prey to a dog is anything that moves that they can attack, such as other animals and children. The question is, how can this be controlled? The best method is to use obedience training. The dog needs to learn that you are in control and dominant over him or her. You can train your dog to resist the urge to chase what it sees as prey.

Curbing aggressive behavior is relative to the amount of training that a dog receives. The more a dog is trained, the less aggressive it will be. The more aggressive a dog is, the more training a dog needs. If you are not comfortable handling training yourself, then it is best to get some professional help.

CHAPTER 2.2: SEPARATION ANXIETY

Separation anxiety is a common problem encountered by many owners and their dogs. Simply defined, separation anxiety is when a dog feels very anxious when left alone. Separation anxiety can present itself in many different ways including chewing, destroying property, excessive barking, self-destructive behavior and inappropriate urination and defecation.

Dogs suffering from separation anxiety often whine, bark, cry, howl, dig, excessively lick themselves, have housebreaking accidents, or chew and scratch at the door the entire time their owners are away. Well-meaning owners often unknowingly encourage this misbehavior by rushing home to reassure their dogs, but it is important for the well-being of both the dog and the owner that the dog learns to deal with extended periods of separation.

Teach your dog to be independent. Do this by discouraging your dog from constantly following you around like a shadow. Train your dog to remain in a down-stay position while you move freely around the house. Start off by leaving the room your dog is in for a few minutes. And then return. Slowly lengthen the times that you are in a different area of the house, separating yourself from your dog. This will help separation anxiety because you are building your dog's confidence. Your dog is learning to be alone yet, he still has the reassurance that you are nearby and will return shortly.

When you do leave your house, how you go about leaving the house often contributes to separation anxiety issues. Do not make a big deal about leaving or returning home. If you act apologetic about leaving your dog, this can actually make your dog more anxious. A long and drawn out farewell with kisses and tearful goodbyes can make matters worse by making your dog feel even more isolated when you finally do leave. Long farewells can also get your dog excited and then leave him or her with lots of excess energy and no way to work it off. Excited, isolated dogs often work off their excess energy by chewing furniture or digging in the yard.

Excess energy is often mistaken for separation anxiety since the results are often the same. If you think that excess amounts of energy may be the problem, try giving your dog more exercise before you leave and see if that eliminates the problem.

If separation anxiety is the true problem, it is important to address the root causes of that anxiety. To prevent separation anxiety, it is important for your dog to feel happy, safe, secure and comfortable while you are away for the day. It is also important to give your dog plenty of things to do to stay occupied while you are away. This means providing lots of toys such as balls, Kong's, or chew toys. A pet companion can also be effective at relieving separation anxiety, like a playmate (in the form of another dog or a cat) can help your dog cope with the stress of being left alone.

Schedule play-time or exercise before your departure and give your dog your undivided attention. Providing your dog with sufficient attention and exercise is a proven way to avoid a stressed and anxious dog. Be sure that you give your dog some time to settle down after playtime or exercise before you leave. A happy dog that has been well exercised and well-conditioned will generally sleep away the time that its owner is away. A tired dog is a good dog.

For dogs that are experiencing separation anxiety and associated misbehaviors it is important to get the dog accustomed to your leaving gradually. Leave your dog home alone for periods of time starting immediately. Practice leaving and returning at irregular intervals, several times a day. If possible, start out with short departures and increase them gradually. Gradually build up to the full amount of time you will be away due to your work or school schedule. Doing this will help your dog realize that you are not leaving him or her forever. Dogs that have been previously lost or those who have been surrendered to shelters and readopted often have the worst problems with separation anxiety. Part of treating this disorder is teaching your dog that your leaving is not permanent.

Dogs that bark incessantly from anxiety become known as nuisance barkers. Nuisance barking can be stopped immediately with the purchase of a bark collar.

If you return home to accidents or damage to your house, this can be upsetting-and the cleanup will rank low in the fun department. It is very important to not discipline or scold your dog for the behaviors committed while you were out. If you do, separation anxiety may become worse because your dog will worry more about you being gone.

If your dog is crate trained, use your dog's crate to assist with dealing with separation anxiety. Crate training is particularly useful if your dog chews or gets into mischief while he is home alone.

Similar to humans, separation anxiety is something that has to be continuously worked on. Stress and the disruption of daily routines can revert a dog to its old behavior.

It is important to understand that correcting separation anxiety is an ongoing process that gets easier as you go along but it is really never cured.

CHAPTER 2.3: NUISANCE BARKING

Unwanted barking is a common problem for dog owners and can be very frustrating for neighbors.

Before you can stop a dog from barking, you need to understand why it barks.

Your dog has a voice and they use its voice to communicate. Barking is not always a bad thing when your dog is using it to talk to you in appropriate situations. However, excessive barking, boredom barking, and nuisance barking is not appropriate and can lead to anger and frustration for owners.

Barking can also depend on the breed of your dog. Guarding breeds such as German Shepherds, Dobermans and Rottweilers were bred to bark when there is a threat. Sporting breeds such as Beagles and Bloodhounds were bred to bark as a tool to assist their owners in seeking a goal. The toy breeds are examples of talkative dogs that bark just to hear themselves.

Discover the Motivation

Dogs bark for many different reasons. Regardless of the breed, there are some circumstances where just about any dog will bark. Some of these are:

- Loneliness
- Bored
- Excited
- Anxious/Nervous
- Hunger, or they know it's meal time
- They want to play
- Something is wrong/someone is near the house
- Needs to go potty
- Sees another animal

It is unrealistic to expect that you can train your dog to completely stop barking for all of the above situations. After all, your dog is a dog and it is in a dog's nature to bark at certain times, at certain things, and in certain situations. A realistic training goal is to curb and control barking when you, the owner, deem it to be uncalled for and inappropriate.

Don't Reinforce It

Your dog may bark excessively because you unintentionally trained it do so, therefore allowing your dog to manipulate you. Your dog barks and you obey. Your dog barks and you open the door to let your dog out. Your dog barks and you open the door to let your dog back in. Your dog barks and the two of you play. Your dog barks and you give it a tummy rub. Your dog has learned to get your attention through barking. It is easy to fall into this trap and it is just as easy to forget to praise and reward your dog when it is not barking.

Yelling and shouting at your dog to stop barking may be negative attention in your mind, but from your dog's point of view, they have your undivided attention, negative or not.

Something else to keep in mind: the more you yell at your dog to stop barking, the more they may bark. This is because they bark, then you bark (yell), and then they bark. Your dog thinks that this is great fun and you are choosing to participate with them.

Desensitization

If your dog's nuisance barking is the result of a specific stimulus, then one technique is to make your dog less sensitive to whatever is causing the barking episode. That can be achieved by exposing the dog to the specific stimulus that triggers the barking repeatedly until it becomes less and less provoking. For example, if your dog goes into a barking fit every time it sees another dog, then try to socialize the dog to be in the presence of other dogs. Get a friend who is a fellow dog owner to bring his or her dog over and slowly let the dogs get to know each other. The more comfortable your dog becomes in the company of other dogs, the less upset it will be when other dogs come into view.

Establish a Quiet Command

It is well known that dogs can be taught to bark on command. What is not so widely known is that they can also be taught to be quiet on command. The first step is to teach your dog to bark when you tell it to speak. This is done by giving the dog a treat every time it barks at your command. Once this relationship between barking on command and getting a treat appears firmly established in your dog's mind, then do the same process to establish a *quiet* command. The key is treats. Once your dog knows that when it is told to stop barking and that when it obeys it will get a treat, you will be surprised by how quickly your dog becomes quiet when it hears the command.

Use a Distraction

When all else fails, one of the best ways to calm a barking dog is to simply distract the animal from whatever is inspiring it to bark. For example: start playing with a ball, or any other interactive activity that will distract the dog. The truth is, the most common cause of nuisance barking is boredom.

Dogs simply have the tendency to bark when they don't know what else to do, so one of the most effective ways of reducing unwanted barking is to keep your dog active. Make sure your dog is getting enough exercise and is not left alone for long periods with nothing to do. A bored dog will often lead to a barking dog, so try to keep your canine's environment stimulating enough so that it is distracted from engaging in nuisance barking.

Always remember that dogs are dogs, and that barking is their way of communicating and expressing their emotions. Therefore you should never expect, nor want your dog to ever stop barking completely.

If you have tried the techniques suggested above and your dog continues to be a nuisance barker, it is time to invest in a bark collar. Bark collars are popular because they are automated and they work. The strategy behind the bark collar is to interrupt the barking behavior with discomfort. The vibration from your dog's vocal cords is what activates the collar. There are three different types of bark collars to choose from. One model emits noise, one blasts air up and into your dog's face, the last uses electrical stimulation.

Which type of bark collar you buy will depend on what you feel the most comfortable with. You should also take into consideration your breed and your dog's sensitivity to pain or sound. A small breed or a dog with a low pain tolerance may respond well to the collar that sprays verses a large breed dog that might only respond to a collar that uses electrical stimulation.

Chapter 2.4: Submissive Urination

Dogs urinate in submission in order to say that they accept the power of a person or another animal, and that they are the submissive one. There is no such thing as spiteful urination, so if your dog is urinating, then there are a number of reasons that they could be urinating. Submissive urination occurs in male dogs as well as female dogs. It is recommended that you make an appointment and take them to veterinarian. To rule out underlying health problems if the problem is frequent.

There are different root causes of submissive urination, but here are a few of the reasons why a dog submissively urinates:

- Excitement
- Low Confidence
- Threatening Behavior

When your dog is submissively urinating, it is important not to yell at or punish your dog. This can even make the problem worse because the dog sees you as an even bigger threat.

Lavish praise and treats on your dog when he goes outside: You want to positively reinforce good behavior and give him food rewards to encourage him to relieve himself outside. This should make the dog want to urinate outside more than when the dog is inside.

Avoid Direct Eye Contact at First

Dogs will sometimes perceive direct eye contact as a threat. For this reason, it is important to avoid direct eye contact with your dog when you first walk into the house or approach your dog.

Speak in Low Tones

When you first walk into the house, your dog is picking up on your demeanor. This is why if you stay calm and low-key when you first walk into the house, you will keep your dog from getting overly excited at your arrival. The tone in your voice lets a dog know how it should react, and if you speak in excited tones, then this can trigger submissive urination.

Don't Grab or Hug the Dog When Walking Into Room

Your dog might see this as a sign of dominance, and as a result they will urinate to show submission. Submissive urination is a common trait in dogs that have been abused or are more timid in nature. It is more common in puppies than in older dogs, but it can also occur in adult dogs.

Urination at a Specific Time

If you find that your dog is urinating submissively at a specific time, then you can restrict your dog's water consumption prior to that time. Be sure that you are taking your dog outdoors on a regular schedule.

Boosting Your Dog's Self-Confidence

Boosting your dog's self-confidence is one way to work on ending submissive urination.

Here are a few suggestions to boost your dog's self-confidence:

- Exercise - exercise works wonders for increasing confidence in dogs, and it allows them to get rid of nervous energy.
- Regular Grooming - like people, dogs feel better about themselves when they are groomed regularly. Regular grooming makes a dog feel loved, which makes him or her healthier, happier and more confident.
- Interactive Games - interact with your dog through play and let him or her win. Play tug-of-war with a rope toy or a rubber ring. ALWAYS let your dog win and then praise him or her lavishly.
- Join a dog training group - a training group can build your dog's confidence through positive training techniques and socialization. You will learn a lot of useful things and you will also meet new and interesting people. You may even find other dog owners who are dealing with the same issues.

Chapter 2.5: Fear Biting

At one point or another in your life, you have witnessed or heard about a dog biting someone out of fear. Man's best friend has feelings and insecurities too and this can cause him or her to bite out of fear. Many times fear biting occurs when a dog is startled or frightened and not properly socialized. It is crucial to recognize and correct this behavior early.

There are many techniques, programs, books and experts that have information on fear biting and how to correct the issue. A few are discussed in this book but know there are many other options available. Dogs, like humans, are unique individuals, so what works for one may not work for all.

The main reasons why dogs bite out of fear are the same faults that cause dogs to be aggressive:

- Poor breeding
- Lack of proper socialization

Socialization is crucial because it helps shape the temperament and character of your dog. A lack of *socialization* also shapes temperament and character, which often results in unwanted behaviors such as aggression and fear biting. If your dog is displaying signs that can lead to biting out of fear, it is your responsibility to work on socializing your dog responsibly. Do not place your dog in situations where they cannot be successful, and do not put other people or dogs at risk.

For example, muzzle your dog to eliminate the possibility of a bite. Enlist some people to help you with meet and greets. Have your helpers stand still with their hands out, without making eye contact with your dog. Walk your dog up to the helper and let your dog initiate the contact. Start out slowly and build from each positive experience. Don't push your dog, or you will agitate instead of correcting the behavior.

Obedience Training

Obedience training and positive reinforcement techniques are a must with all breeds of all ages and sizes. Obedience cannot be stressed enough if you have a dog that is prone to anxiousness and fearful behavior. Obedience reinforces your leadership and pack status over your dog. In uncertain situations it is crucial that you be able to control and direct your dog. Obedience training will also build your dog's confidence and trust and can be used to distract your dog's attention away from potentially negative behaviors or circumstances before they occur.

Train Your Family Members

The dog is not the only one that needs to be trained. It is important to teach children of all ages not to sneak up on the dog, not to roughhouse or dominate the dog in play, and to teach everyone to use the same training techniques and commands you are using to promote consistency. Adults need to be trained to not be overbearing around a dog with fear issues. Do not regularly greet the dog in a dominant position such as standing or leaning over the dog. This body language can put a lot of pressure on an insecure dog. Instead keep your body language neutral and be friendly, playful and loving with your tone of voice.

Your Reaction

Your reaction to the things that cause your dog's anxiety or fear may be eliciting and encouraging negative responses. Be sure you are calm and show no signs of fear or worry in situations that could lead to fear biting. Your dog will cue and feed off of you. When you notice signs from your pet that he may be getting anxious or fearful, remain calm and take charge of the situation. It is your responsibility to read your dog and redirect his attention or remove your dog from a situation.

Recognize

Try to recognize what is causing your dog's fear. As the dog goes through various stages of development there is a fear imprint stage. If this feeling of fear is not abated, the dog may associate that fear with a similar situation in the future. For instance, if the mailman startled the dog as a puppy while he was sleeping, the dog may be afraid of anyone in a uniform. Anytime the UPS delivery person, or the plumber shows up, your dog may associate that person in a uniform with the time he was first startled and react in the same way. If you recognize what the fear is, you can work on easing and correcting the fear before the situation gets out of hand.

History

Try to learn as much about your pet as you can. If you are purchasing/adopting a rescue pet, try to find out if he or she has been abused. You will need to spend a lot of time with your new pet to get to learn his or her attitudes, personality and characteristics. Not all pets that have bitten before will bite again as long as they have the proper corrective training. If possible, get the background history on the dogs parents. Biting is not an inherent trait but it can be a learned behavior if the parents were fearful as well.

The best thing you can do for your pet is to love it and give it a secure home environment. Provide your pet with a well-balanced diet, a regular eating schedule, exercise on a regular basis, lots of love, positive attention, and boundaries. You will be providing your pet with a healthy life and regular routines, thus reducing the level of anxiety and fear that he may have experienced in the past.

Know your dog and do not take unnecessary chances. If your dog is questionable around company, be a responsible pet owner and do not put your guests and your dog into a potential situation. Your dog might behave wonderfully but why risk it? Seclude your dog in another part of the house where your dog is comfortable and you are free to enjoy your company.

Dogs become a member of the family, and they need care and compassion. If they are experiencing issues, you need to understand these issues and attempt the best possible solutions to help. One remedy may not be enough for your pet; you may need to try several before you find the combination that works.

CHAPTER 2.6: DIGGING

Digging is an annoying negative behavioral trait your canine companion can have. The result is ruined flowerbeds and holes under fencing, which can lead to fines from the local animal control authorities because the dog is roaming the neighborhood and is being a nuisance.

The good news is that there are preventative measures you can take to help alleviate this annoying behavior. The bad news is that it is going to take some effort on your part as the responsible pet owner to correct the problem.

The first and most important question that an owner of a dog with digging issues should ask is: Why is the dog digging? Terriers, for example, were bred specifically to dig various things up for their owners. Other breeds, such as larger working breeds, were bred for herding or protection work, so digging for them has more to do with boredom and sheer restlessness.

It is important to understand that digging is an instinctive behavior for dogs. Your dog's desire to dig is healthy and normal. It is a dog's natural instinct to hide a bone or some other small item that is his. Let your dog have his little secret stash and observe how ritualistic your dog is about how and where it will hide or bury its bones (if allowed).

Problem digging is always the result of your dog being bored.

Owners often have no option but to leave their dog at home alone during the day while the family is out either working or attending school. Your dog becomes bored while home alone and it looks for entertaining ways to pass the time. Digging is one favorite pastime.

How to cope with canine boredom

All dogs need exercise. The larger and more active the breed, the more exercise and play-time they are going to require. Daily walks, daily runs, Frisbee and ball time are essentials for keeping your dog healthy, happy and tired.

It is important to make sure your pet has enough chew toys, treats and diversions to stay stimulated, entertained and out of trouble.

If your dog suffers from separation anxiety, it may dig to alleviate stress and anxiety. Your stressed dog may also dig under the fence and out of the yard to search for you because they fear you are never, coming back home.

If your dog destroys landscaping from destructive digging, do not replace the area if you do not plan on relocating the dog to a different area of the yard or plan on kenneling him. This only sets you and your dog up for failure. Your dog will repeat the destructive digging behavior as many times as you replace the landscaping.

Crating and kenneling a dog on a concrete slab will immediately control the digging behavior. Some owners prefer to keep their dogs outdoors for the protection purposes of their property.

Digging is a behavior that is hard to stop if you leave your dog outside unattended for extended periods of time. Occasional digging issues can be stopped by removing temptations, removing your dog from the environment, and catching your dog digging in the act and discouraging the behavior.

CHAPTER 3: CLICKER TRAINING

Clicker training is a fun, easy, cruelty-free training method that generally achieves good results with dogs of any age, even puppies. Dogs can be taught a variety of commands and the clicker can be worked by people of all ages and sizes.

Any member of your family can get your dog or puppy to obey their command. There is no need to physically discipline your dog because the click itself becomes the reward. The only negative reinforcement this method uses is the lack of a click when your dog does not perform whatever task you are asking. This is a safe, kind method of teaching your dog good manners.

All that is required to clicker train your pet is a clicker, some patience, and some yummy treats for positive reinforcement.

The average clicker training device is inexpensive and can be purchased in most pet stores or online. I recommend buying more than one to have available in multiple locations.

CHAPTER 3.1: TIPS ON HOW TO USE CLICKER TRAINING

One of the best ways an owner can begin to build a relationship with his or her dog is through obedience training. Consistent training will build a bond and a level of trust between you and your dog.

The clicker is a small hand held plastic box with a metal strip inside that makes a distinct "clicking" sound when pressed.

Clicker training is a form of conditioning. The sound of the clicker is used to trigger a positive reaction in your dog. The advantage of using a clicker is that it is faster and more distinct than saying "good dog." The clicker is more effective than your voice because the distinct noise your dog hears will be followed closely with a reward. This causes your dog to associate the clicking noise with positive attention and upcoming treats.

Timing

The secret to the success of any training technique is timing and consistency. You, the human, are the key ingredient when it comes to these two factors. When clicker training your dog, you must learn to time the positive reinforcement (click + treat) with the desired behavior. If the click is too early or too late, there is the possibility of confusing your dog as to what you want him or her to do. Do not click as you give a command but do click and immediately treat as soon as your dog performs the command. For example, tell your dog "sit." As soon as he sits, immediately click and treat.

Treats

Treats are initially the incentive behind your dog's motivation and performance. In the early stages of clicker training it is imperative every click is followed by a treat. This creates an association between the click and a treat. Your dog performs the desired behavior, you click and immediately treat. Repeat this over and over and before you know it, your dog will be eager to hear the clicker sound.

"Length" of a Click

There will be times when you want to give your dog some extra attention for a job well done. When this happens do not click multiple times but instead hold the button to prolong the gap between the first and second click. (The clicker button usually makes a small noise at both the press and the release.) Then proceed to give your dog a bit more praise and treats compared to the usual routine.

Multiple Clicks

This ties into advice offered in the last section in regards to how many times to click. It is important to remember while using the clicker that each click should relate to one action at a time. If your dog is performing a number of separate tricks, or simply demonstrating a series of behaviors that you wish to encourage, then it is appropriate to click the number of times in correspondence to each of those actions. Otherwise make sure that you are only giving one click if only one action is being performed.

Ignore Bad Behavior

In contrast to verbal scolding, silence is a good counteracting tool to remedy unwanted behavior. Dogs, like people, respond to attention. However, for most dogs, any attention, including negative attention, is good attention. Ignoring bad or unwanted behavior does not acknowledge your dog with the response or the attention he desires. To work towards ending bad behavior, keep your clicker with you at all times and be ready to click and reward good behavior. Positively reinforce good behavior and ignore bad and unwanted behavior. Your dog will soon be inclined to exemplify behavior that earns a click rather than behavior that earns no response at all.

Lengths of the Training Session

As with all training methods, keep your training sessions short. Dogs have short attention spans and you want them focused during training. Five to ten minute sessions a couple of times a day will produce better results compared to training every day for an hour.

With many options available to help you train your dog to be an obedient companion, clicker training is an excellent choice. There is little expense and dogs and puppies react very positively to this type of training. Get your training supplies lined up and get started clicking your way to a well-mannered pet.

CHAPTER 4: GET TO CRATE TRAINING

Keeping your dog safe and secure is one of your chief responsibilities as a dog owner. Crate training your dog is an invaluable tool that can help. If your dog is having issues with separation anxiety, chewing, housebreaking, or cannot yet be trusted when out of your sight, a crate is the answer to your prayers and sanity.

Crate training may take a few weeks to a few months depending on the personality and the age of the dog. Be prepared for some whining, howling or barking, but it will pass-don't give in to it.

Why Crate Train

Dogs are innately den and territorial animals that need to have a safe space that is their own. Having that space encourages a sense of security in your dog. The idea behind crate training is that you provide your dog with a place where it can go to sleep, relax or just get away from the hustle and bustle of your household. The crate becomes not only your dog's bed, but also a secure place where you can contain him and keep him out of harm's way when needed.

Allowing your dog to spend time in his crate every day can also aid in the housebreaking process. In general, dogs will not soil the place where they sleep. This goes back to the mother dog's instinct to keep her puppies safe. By crate training your dog, and making his crate the place where he sleeps, you are establishing a "no potty zone" for him. Eventually, dogs and puppies can be taught to expand the no-go zone to a room and then ultimately to your entire home. Through the use of crate training you will find that your dog can be house broken in almost no time at all.

Used properly, crate training can help your dog to become a well-behaved, well-adjusted member of your family. In times when you need to confine your dog, sending him to his crate is an ideal choice. In times when your dog is uncomfortable with whatever is going on in your home, he will willingly and happily retreat to his crate. If you bring your dog's crate with you when you travel even the most unfamiliar location will feel secure to him, which will encourage good behavior.

Getting Started with Crate Training

Many people mistakenly believe that crate training is nothing more than locking your dog up when he or she does something wrong. This is not the case. Crate training is actually more about teaching your dog that it has a space of its own. Although you may place your dog in the crate when it does something inappropriate, dogs should also spend time there throughout the day so that they do not associate the crate with punishment. Many pet owners are pleasantly surprised to discover that their dogs learn to love their crates and that they seek them out on their own.

Crate training should be a positive experience and should never be used for punishment. When you first bring home the crate or the dog, make the crate enticing with bedding, toys and treats, and encourage the dog to enter the crate and explore. When you are not crating your dog, always leave the door open so that he has the option to enter and exit as he pleases.

When first starting out, introduce the crate slowly, only leaving your dog in the crate for a few minutes at a time and always stay within your dog's view so that it does not feel abandoned. As your dog becomes accustomed to the crate, gradually increase the amount of time he is crated. Also work on coming and going from the area where the dog is crated so he becomes accustomed to being alone.

You will need to choose a command or a phrase to cue your dog to get in the crate. Some examples are: "crate," "kennel" or "get in your house." When your dog goes into the crate, give verbal praise (such as "good kennel"). Close the door and give him a treat. When your dog has finished the treat, calmly open the door and let him out of the crate.

Never remove your dog from the crate if it is whining, howling, digging or barking. Ignore this behavior and only remove your dog after it has quieted down. Never reward unwanted behavior.

Always remember to praise and reward your dog when it enters the crate, but never upon exit. It is important to remain nonchalant when you release your dog from the crate. Save the excitement for outside of the crate.

It will not take long before your dog is comfortable and confident inside of his or her crate.

Tips for success:

The crate needs to be large enough for the dog to comfortably stand up, turn around and stretch out.

Smaller dogs need smaller crates to maximize comfort.

Exercise your dog before crating for an extended period of time. A tired dog will nap eliminating boredom and anxiety.

Start slowly and gradually increase the time spent in the crate.

Puppies can only hold their bladder (on average) for 3-4 hours. Do not crate them longer than this.

Chapter 5: The Art Of Positive Reinforcement

It is widely accepted among the vast majority of dog training experts that the easiest, most successful and humane way to train your dog is through positive reinforcement training. The theory behind the positive reinforcement method is easy. Dogs love to be praised and given attention. This is an asset when training a dog. Using positive reinforcement involves rewarding the behavior that you wish to see repeated, and ignoring the behavior that you do not. When we call our dogs we praise them when they come to us. This is an example of positive reinforcement.

Positive reinforcement is a method in direct contrast to some of the now outdated but once popular techniques for dog training. The theory of positive reinforcement is that lessons are more meaningful to dogs and will tend to stick better when a dog is able to figure out on its own what you are asking it to do. This is in contrast to, for example, a dog learning the down command by being forced repeatedly into a prone position while the word "down" is repeated at intervals.

When you use positive reinforcement training, you are allowing your dog the time and the opportunity to use his or her own brain. To make the training process easier and more rewarding, you need to use meaningful rewards. Dogs get bored pretty quickly with a routine pat on the head and a "good doggy." Keep the quality of your dog's learning at a high standard by using tempting incentives for good behavior. Food treats and physical affection are what dog trainers refer to as "primary incentives." They are both significant rewards that most dogs respond powerfully and reliably to.

Every dog is different, and not all dogs are driven by food. If your dog is not food motivated, verbal praise alone will only go so far for so long. Figure out what motivates your dog. The item needs to be something he wants badly and will work for. If it is a favorite toy, use this toy *only* for reward and positive behavior. This will build your dog's desire for the toy and he will quickly learn that he has to earn the toy through positive behavior.

Be sure to shower your dog with a lot of praise and positive attention for positive behavior even when you are not training in a structured setting. During the early stages of training, you are shaping and molding your dog's behavior, even if you don't realize it. Dogs generally want to please, they are ready to learn, and they pick up on verbal and non-verbal cues from their owners. Positive rewards and attention encourage positive behavior no matter the place or setting. Your dog will thrive knowing that he has done well and will continue to want to please you.

Be sure to use rewards consistently. It is also important to be consistent with your training commands. When you are teaching a dog a command, you need to decide ahead of time on the verbal cue you are going to use and then stick to it. So, when training your dog to not jump up on you, for example, do not use "get off," "get down," and "stop jumping," interchangeably. Pick one phrase such as "no jumping," and stick with it to avoid confusion. Even the smartest dogs learn most quickly through consistent repetition, (in this case, the actions associated with a particular phrase). Using consistent commands and treats to reinforce positive behavior makes training less confusing and makes desired results happen faster.

The great perk about positive reinforcement training is that it does not require you to undertake any harsh punitive measures if your dog exhibits unwanted behavior. All you have to do is ignore the behavior. Not getting attention is enough to make just about any dog miserable. This alone is a powerful correctional tool.

Contemporary belief in dog training states that we should simply ignore incorrect responses to a training command. With no reinforcement from us, positive or negative, your dog will stop the behavior on its own. Remember that negative attention like verbal corrections count as reinforcement. To some dogs, negative attention is better than no attention at all. The bigger the fuss you make over your dog when it does something right, the clearer the distinction will be between positive and negative behaviors.

Ignoring bad behavior is not always realistic when you are in the early stages of training. For example: you want your dog to alert and bark when the doorbell rings, which is initially a desired behavior (and instinctual for most breeds). But now that you are at the door, you want your dog to stop barking so you can open the door. In this situation, you need to answer the door and do not have the luxury to ignore your dog's barking (undesired behavior) until he stops.

There are many things that will pop up on a daily basis that will initially set you and your dog up for failure. Deal with the situation as best as you can in the moment and make a mental note of the problem or behavior you need work on.

Let's use our barking example. To teach a dog to stop barking, you must first teach it to bark on command. Choose a bark command such as *speak*. Hold a treat so your dog can see it or smell it; then give the command "speak." Continue to give the command. Your dog will likely become frustrated because he or she wants the treat, but the dog does not understand what you want. When the dog emits any noise such as whimpering or whining, immediately reward with the treat and verbal praise: "good speak." This is the process of shaping their behavior. Continue this process until your dog associates the command *speak* with barking. This may take several sessions.

When your dog understands and can perform speak on command, it is time to teach your dog to stop barking. Choose a no-bark command such as *quiet*. Give your dog the *bark* command and let him bark. Now give the quiet command. You will need to calmly repeat the command until he stops barking. Immediately reward with a treat and verbal praise: "good quiet." Continue this process until your dog understands the quiet command.

The next step in our example is to purposely set your dog up for failure so you can be in control of successfully shaping the desired behavior. Ask someone to ring your doorbell. This scenario is a training session to enforce the quiet command. You will not reward your dog or open the door until your dog has performed the behavior that you desire from him. (How your dog responds and behaves when the door is opened is a separate training issue.) Repeat this training scenario until you are happy and confident with the results.

When you are not in training mode, be careful not to reinforce bad behavior. This can be difficult. Until you catch yourself doing it, you may not even realize it's happening. Any behavior from your dog that initiates a scolding or negative attention is reinforcing bad behavior. Be aware of your actions and reactions and understand that training a dog is not just about molding and shaping a dog's behavior but also the owner's behavior.

When training a dog remember the following tips:

- Keep your training sessions short and fun
- Commands need to be short and concise
- Don't be stingy with rewards, verbal praise and affection when they are well deserved
- Be consistent and ask others in the family to do the same
- Positive reinforcement = good behavior
- Good behavior = a happy, well-mannered pet

Identify your training goals and address current issues and new problems and challenges as they present themselves. Patience, determination, and consistency combined with the right training techniques will result in a successfully trained and well-mannered dog.

CHAPTER 6: BEST TRAINING TIPS BY BREED

Training a dog can sometimes be an overwhelming process. It can also bond and really connect an owner with his or her animal. How well the process goes depends on consistency and commitment when training the dog. No matter what the breed, striking an animal is never appropriate. Always use a firm tone of voice, and reward positive behavior instead of punishing negative behavior. This chapter presents specific training tips for various breeds.

Training Tips for a Beagle

These dogs need adequate socialization with people and other dogs or they may become aggressive. Remember that beagles hunt by scent and are easily influenced by various smells.

Training Tips for a Bulldog

American Bulldogs can be aggressive. Start obedience training at a young age. English Bulldogs love to eat. Treats to reinforce good behavior work well with this breed. Don't go overboard. English

Bulldogs are prone to obesity and need to be walked regularly.

Training Tips for a Chihuahua

Socialization is crucial to properly train a Chihuahua. They can become suspicious of new people and are not always comfortable around small children. These dogs are small, making it easy to control this breed on a leash.

Training Tips for a Cocker Spaniel

Cocker Spaniels love people and need lots of attention. They also have a tendency to have bladder issues and may relieve themselves if they get too excited. Crate training is a good method to use when training a Cocker Spaniel.

Training Tips for a Collie

Keep in mind that Collies are herding dogs. They naturally want to round up things that are moving. To keep a Collie from chasing cars, bicycles, and small children, train this breed early using a leash. Collies are intelligent and eager to please their owners. It is usually not difficult to reign in their natural tendencies with strong obedience and leash training.

Training Tips for a Dalmatian

Dalmatians should be trained as early as possible. This breed is active and known to be destructive through chewing. Providing the Dalmatian with lots of chew toys is essential. Do not expect a Dalmatian to reach maturity until about two years of age.

Training Tips for a German Shepherd

German Shepherds are fearless, intelligent dogs often used in police work. Most are ready to begin training as young as seven or eight weeks old. Training these dogs through tricks and exercises are good ways to stimulate them both physically and mentally.

Training Tips for a Golden Retriever

Golden Retrievers do well in an established routine. Establish where the dog is to eat and sleep as soon as possible. Socialize this breed as much as possible while young. A Golden Retriever may be cute and cuddly to sleep with as a puppy, but be aware that fully grown versions are large-and they shed.

Training Tips for a Great Dane

Great Danes need to walk and be exercised on a daily basis. It is good to have a handle on the heel command since Danes are such a large breed. Despite their size and stern look, Great Danes are sensitive dogs. Refrain from being too stern with Great Danes when training them. It is not recommended to teach Great Danes to roll over because they have a deep chest cavity and are prone to a condition called gastric torsion.

Training Tips for an Irish Setter

Irish Setters need a lot of mental and physical stimulation. Mental and physical activity needs to be part of their training process or they may get bored and become destructive. It may be difficult to housebreak some Irish Setters. Being patient and keeping the dog on a frequent and regular schedule is crucial.

Training Tips for a Labrador Retriever

Labs are energetic and crave lots of attention. When training them make sure to incorporate physical activity into the routine. This breed instinctively likes to hold items in their mouths. To keep a Lab from taking the throw pillows off the furniture, provide them with plenty of plush toys.

Training Tips for a Maltese

These dogs are small and need to be walked only 10 to 15 minutes at a clip. Maltese often form strong bonds with their owners and may suffer from separation anxiety. Proper crate training may reduce this behavior.

Training Tips for a Poodle

Poodles can be stubborn. Keeping distractions to a minimum is crucial so the dog can stay focused. If the dog is having a difficult day it may be best to stop training and start again at another time.

Training Tips for a Shetland Sheepdog

Like Collies, these dogs are natural herders. Leash training should begin early. They must be taught at a young age not to chase after everything that moves. Since they are smaller than Collies they may need to relieve themselves more often, and they should be taken out frequently for potty breaks.

Training Tips for a Terrier

All Terriers can be difficult to train. You need an authoritative firmness and you need to establish very early that you are the boss. That lets this breed know that you rank above him in the pack structure. Don't give a terrier a treat for free in the initial stages of training. Only use treats as rewards for positive behavior.

MEET THE AUTHOR

Amy and Bruno

Amy Morford has over twenty years of dog training experience with companion dogs, sport dogs and working breeds. Amy's motivation to write about dogs stems from her love for them and their unbiased loyalty and devotion. Amy's goal is to provide helpful, accurate information to assist dog lovers with raising and training a well-mannered, good-tempered, happy, healthy, well-adjusted companion, friend, partner and/or family pet.

More Books by Amy Morford

Dog Eldercare: Caring For Your Middle-Aged To Older Dog

DoggyPedia: All You Need To Know About Dogs

Dog Quotes: Proverbs, Quotes & Quips

Pet Names and Numerology: Choose the Right Name For Your Pet

Puppy Training: From Day 1 to Adulthood (How to Make Your Puppy Loving and Obedient)

Scared Dog Audio

The German Shepherd Big Book: All About The German Shepherd Breed

www.ingramcontent.com/pod-product-compliance
Ingram Content Group UK Ltd.
Pitfield, Milton Keynes, MK11 3LW, UK
UKHW022120230426
12048UKWH00010BA/620